THE ULTIMATE
Bees
BOOK FOR KIDS

BELLANOVA

MELBOURNE · SOFIA · BERLIN

© 2026 by Jenny Kellett
Bees: The Ultimate Bee Book
www.bellanovabooks.com

All rights reserved. No part of this book may be reproduced in any form by any electronic or mechanical means including photocopying, recording, or information storage and retrieval without permission in writing from the author.

Imprint: Bellanova Books
ISBN: 978-619-264-147-4

Contents

Introduction 4
The Life of Bees 8
Bee Anatomy 15
Bee Species 23
The Beehive 31
    The Queen Bee 38
    Worker bees 42
    Drones 49
    Solitary bees 54
Honey 57
Pollination 65
Threats to bees 69
Bee Fun Facts 74
The Bee Quiz 92
Answers 96
Word search 99
    Solution 100
Sources 101
Also by Jenny Kellett 104

Introduction

Welcome, bee lovers, to *Bees: The Ultimate Book*! We're so glad you've joined us on this exciting adventure to learn all about the buzzing world of bees. If you've ever seen a bee buzz by or heard one humming around a flower, you know how fascinating these tiny creatures can be. Did you know there are more than 20,000 different species of bees in the world? Wow! And they come in all sorts of colors, shapes, and sizes. In this book, we're going to explore the fantastic lives of these hardworking insects and discover just how important they are to our planet.

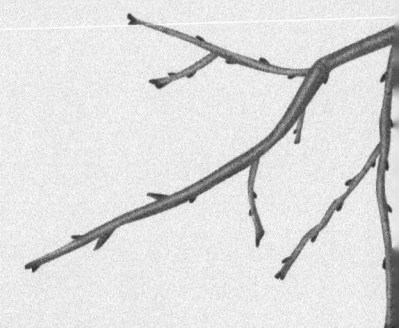

BEE SUPERPOWERS

Bees are incredible creatures with superpowers you may not even realize. They can fly long distances, find their way home without a GPS, and even communicate with each other through amazing dances. Plus, they're master builders, creating intricate homes called **hives**. But their most important job is to help plants grow by pollinating them. Without bees, we wouldn't have many of our favorite fruits, veggies, and nuts.

MEETING THE BEE FAMILY

Throughout this book, we'll take a closer look at the many types of bees buzzing around our planet. From the well-known honeybee to the fuzzy bumblebee, and even the mysterious solitary bees, there's so much to learn about these incredible insects. We'll dive into the life of a bee, explore their homes and jobs, and learn how they communicate with each other. And we'll find out how bees create delicious honey, which humans have been enjoying for thousands of years.

PROTECTING OUR BEE FRIENDS

But bees need our help, too. They're facing some tough challenges these days, like losing their homes and dealing with pollution. We'll learn what we can do to help protect these amazing creatures and keep them buzzing for years to come.

READY, SET, BUZZ!

So, are you ready to start your journey into the world of bees? Great! Let's get buzzing and discover the fascinating secrets of these tiny superheroes that play such a huge role in our lives. On to Chapter 2, where we'll explore the life of a bee, from its very beginning as a tiny egg to its busy life as an adult!

The Life of Bees

Let's dive into the fascinating life cycle of a bee, from its start as a tiny egg to its buzzing life as an adult. We'll discover the many changes bees go through as they grow, and learn about the incredible transformation they experience during their lives. So, let's get started on our journey through the life of a bee!

THE ULTIMATE BEE BOOK

EGGS-TRAORDINARY BEGINNINGS

Our story starts inside the hive, where the queen bee lays her eggs in special cells made of wax. Each egg is about the size of a pinhead - so tiny! The queen bee can lay up to 2,000 eggs in a single day. That's a lot of future bees!

THE GROWING LARVAE

After three to four days, the eggs hatch into little white larvae, which look like tiny worms. The worker bees feed the larvae a special mix of pollen, nectar, and a substance called "**royal jelly**." This superfood helps the larvae grow quickly, molting (shedding their skin) several times during this stage.

COCOONING IN THE PUPAL STAGE

About a week later, the worker bees seal the larvae's cells with wax, and the larvae spin themselves a cozy cocoon. Inside their cocoons, the larvae transform into **pupae**. This stage is called the "pupal" stage. It's like magic! Their bodies change shape, and they start to develop wings, legs, and other adult bee features.

BEE-COMING AN ADULT

After about two to three weeks, depending on the species, the fully-formed adult bee chews its way out of the wax cell. It's now ready to join the rest of the hive and begin its life as a buzzing, hardworking member of the colony.

A female gray mining bee.

FINDING THEIR PLACE IN THE HIVE

As adult bees, they have different roles in the colony depending on their age and type. Worker bees, which are all female, take on various tasks like cleaning, nursing, guarding, and foraging. Male bees, called drones, have only one job: to mate with a queen bee. And the queen bee, of course, lays the eggs that will grow into the next generation of bees.

THE END OF A BEE'S JOURNEY

A bee's life span depends on its species and role in the colony. Worker bees usually live for several weeks to a few months, while drones live only until they mate with a queen or until the end of the season when they are kicked out of the hive. Queen bees, on the other hand, can live for several years, laying millions of eggs during their lifetime.

THE ULTIMATE BEE BOOK

Bee Anatomy

In this chapter, we'll get up close and personal with our buzzing buddies to explore the fascinating world of bee anatomy. From their fuzzy bodies to their incredible wings, bees are truly amazing creatures. So, grab your magnifying glass and let's take a closer look at the parts that make up a bee!

HEAD: THE COMMAND CENTER

The head is where all the action begins! Bees have two large compound eyes, made up of thousands of tiny lenses called **ommatidia**. These eyes help them see colors, patterns, and even ultraviolet light that we humans can't see. Between their compound eyes, bees also have three small, simple eyes called **ocelli**, which help them detect light and movement.

A bee's mouth is like a multi-tool. They have **mandibles** (jaws) to bite and chew, as well as a **proboscis** (a long, flexible tongue) to sip nectar from flowers. On their head, they also have a pair of **antennae**, which act like tiny feelers to help them smell, taste, and touch the world around them.

THORAX & ABDOMEN

The thorax is the bee's powerhouse, where their wings and legs are attached. Bees have two pairs of wings - a larger front pair and a smaller back pair.

When they fly, they hook their wings together, making them work as one large, powerful set of wings. Bees are excellent fliers, able to fly up to 15 miles per hour (24 km/h) and they can even hover in place!

Attached to the thorax, bees also have three pairs of legs. Each leg has a special function, like collecting pollen or helping them grip onto surfaces. The back legs of many bees, especially worker honeybees, have pollen baskets called **corbiculae**. These are like tiny saddlebags, used to carry pollen back to the hive.

The abdomen is the largest part of a bee's body and contains many important organs. Inside, there's a **honey stomach** (a special pouch just for storing nectar), the digestive system, and the reproductive organs. The abdomen also holds the stinger, which is a special egg-laying organ called an **ovipositor**. Only female bees (worker bees and queen bees) have stingers, while male bees (drones) do not.

FUZZY FASHION

Bees are often covered in **fuzz**, which helps them collect pollen and stay warm. This fuzz can come in various colors, like black, yellow, orange, or even white. Some bees, like honeybees and bumblebees, have distinct stripes, while others, like carpenter bees, are mostly one color. Each species has its own unique pattern, making them easy to identify.

A mining bee.

An orange-tailed mining bee.

A bumblebee.

A honey bee.

Bee Species

Did you know that there are over 20,000 different species of bees?! That's right—there's so much to discover about these buzzing wonders. Each species has its own unique traits, habits, and roles in the ecosystem. From the smallest Perdita bee to the giant Wallace's giant bee, there's so much diversity in the world of bees!

So, let's learn more about just a few examples of the thousands of bee species out there.

THE ULTIMATE BEE BOOK

HONEY BEES

When most people think of bees, they think of honeybees. These social insects live in large colonies and are famous for making delicious honey. Honeybees (*scientific name: Apis mellifera*) come in various colors, from golden brown to nearly black. They're important pollinators and are often used by farmers to help their crops grow.

BUMBLEBEES

Bumblebees (*scientific name: bombus*) are easy to recognize with their big, fuzzy bodies and distinctive black and yellow stripes. There are over 250 species of bumblebees!

They're social insects, living in smaller colonies than honeybees. Bumblebees are also excellent pollinators, using a technique called **"buzz pollination"** to shake pollen loose from flowers by vibrating their wings super fast.

THE ULTIMATE BEE BOOK

CARPENTER BEES

Carpenter bees (*scientific name: Xylocopa*) are solitary bees that come in a wide range of sizes and colors. Carpenter bees are usually less fuzzy than other bees and have a shiny abdomen. Carpenter bees are named for their ability to drill holes in wood to make their nests.

A tropical carpenter bee.
© Charles J. Sharp

© André Karwath

MASON BEES

Mason bees (*scientific name: Osmia*) are small, solitary bees known for their incredible nest-building skills. They use mud to build their nests in small cracks or crevices, earning them the name "mason" bees. These gentle bees come in various colors, like metallic green, blue, or black. Mason bees are fantastic pollinators and are becoming more popular in gardens and orchards.

LEAFCUTTER BEES

Leafcutter bees (*scientific name: Megachilidae*) are another type of solitary bee, famous for their unique nest-building technique. They cut small pieces of leaves or petals to line their nests, which they build in hollow stems or holes in wood. Leafcutter bees are important pollinators, and you might even spot them in your own garden!

SWEAT BEES

Sweat bees (*scientific name: Halictidae*) are the second-largest family of bees. They are small, often metallic-colored bees that get their name because they're attracted to human sweat. Don't worry, they're generally harmless! These bees can be social or solitary, depending on the species. They're important pollinators for many wildflowers and crops.

Home sweet home:
The Beehive

Now it's time to take an exciting journey into the heart of the beehive, the home of our buzzing friends. We'll learn about how bees build their incredible homes and the different roles bees play within the hive.

THE HIVE: A BUZZING COMMUNITY

A beehive is a lot like a bustling city, with each bee working together to create a safe, thriving community. Most beehives are made by social bees, like honeybees and bumblebees, who live together in large groups called colonies. Hives can be found in various locations, from hollow trees to human-made bee boxes.

THE BUILDING BLOCKS: BEESWAX AND MORE

Bees are master builders, creating their homes from wax and other materials. Honeybees produce beeswax from special glands in their abdomen. They then use their mandibles (jaws) to shape the wax into hexagonal cells. These cells form the honeycomb, which is the main structure of the hive.

Bumblebees, on the other hand, create their nests from a mix of wax, plant materials, and even abandoned animal burrows. Their homes may not be as organized as honeybees' hives, but they're just as cozy and functional.

A PLACE FOR EVERYTHING: HIVE ORGANIZATION

Within the hive, there's a place for everything. Honeycomb cells are used for various purposes, like storing honey, pollen, and raising baby bees (**brood**). In honeybee hives, the brood cells are usually located in the center, surrounded by pollen storage cells, with honey storage cells near the top and edges.

Bumblebee nests are a bit more relaxed in organization. They have small waxen pots for storing nectar and pollen, and brood cells where the queen lays her eggs.

A natural honeybee hive.

ROLES WITHIN THE HIVE

Each bee in the colony has a specific role to play. Here's a quick rundown of the main roles in a beehive:

Queen Bee: The queen is the mother of the colony. Her main job is to lay eggs, ensuring the colony's future. There's usually only one queen per hive.

Worker Bees: Worker bees are all female and do most of the foraging, nursing, cleaning, and guarding. As they age, their roles within the hive change.

Drones: These male bees have one purpose - to mate with a queen. They don't have stingers and can't forage for food, relying on the worker bees to feed them.

KEEPING THINGS COOL: HIVE TEMPERATURE CONTROL

Bees are experts at maintaining the perfect temperature in their hive. Honeybees use their wings to fan the air, creating a cooling breeze. They also collect water and spread it throughout the hive, which evaporates and helps lower the temperature. In the winter, they cluster together and use their body heat to keep the hive warm.

And that's our tour of the beehive, a bee's home sweet home! These amazing insects work together to create a safe, thriving community that supports the entire colony. In the next chapter, we'll focus on the life and importance of the queen bee, the mother of the colony. Get ready to meet the queen!

THE ULTIMATE BEE BOOK

The Queen Bee

The queen bee is the one and only mother of the colony. Let's learn about her unique upbringing, her royal duties, and how she keeps the colony running smoothly.

A ROYAL BEGINNING

The queen bee starts her life just like any other bee: as an egg laid by the current queen in a special cell within the hive. However, not all eggs are destined to become queens. Only the eggs that are fed a unique diet of royal jelly throughout their entire larval stage will grow into queen bees. This royal jelly is a special substance produced by worker bees that is packed with nutrients, helping the queen larva grow larger and develop differently than other bees. When the queen larva is ready to pupate, her cell is capped, and she spins a cocoon to complete her transformation.

THE CORONATION: BECOMING THE QUEEN

Once the new queen bee emerges from her cell, her first order of business is to establish her reign. If there are other newly-emerged queens in the hive, they may fight to the death to determine who will rule. The winner will become the one and only queen of the colony.

After asserting her dominance, the new queen will take her mating flights. She mates with multiple drones (male bees) in mid-air, storing their sperm in a special organ called the **spermatheca**. Once she has mated, she'll have enough sperm to lay eggs for the rest of her life.

THE QUEEN'S ROYAL DUTIES

As the mother of the colony, the queen bee's main job is to lay eggs - lots and lots of eggs! A healthy queen can lay up to 2,000 eggs per day during peak season. She uses her stored sperm to fertilize her eggs, producing female worker bees and future queens. Unfertilized eggs will develop into male drones.

The queen also plays a crucial role in maintaining harmony within the hive. She produces **pheromones**, chemical scents that help regulate the behavior of the worker bees. These pheromones prevent worker bees from laying their own eggs and encourage them to work together as a team.

A QUEEN'S REIGN

A queen bee's life can last for several years, much longer than the life of a worker bee or drone. Throughout her life, the queen will continue to lay eggs and produce pheromones,

ensuring the survival and success of her colony. When her egg-laying abilities decline or she dies, a new queen will take her place, continuing the cycle of life in the beehive.

The queen bee plays a vital role in keeping the colony thriving and ensuring its future.

worker bees

It's time to shine a spotlight on the true heroes of the beehive: worker bees. These hardworking ladies do it all, from foraging for food to caring for the young. So, let's dive into the busy life of worker bees and learn about their many roles and responsibilities!

THE MANY HATS OF WORKER BEES

Worker bees are all female, and they make up the majority of the bees in a colony. They perform a wide range of tasks to keep the hive running smoothly. As worker bees age, their roles within the hive change. They typically start with tasks inside the hive and gradually move to foraging duties as they get older.

NURSE BEES: CARING FOR THE NEXT GENERATION

When worker bees are just a few days old, they begin their duties as nurse bees. Nurse bees are responsible for feeding and caring for the brood - the developing larvae and pupae. They produce a special food called **brood food**, a mix of honey, pollen, and glandular secretions, which they feed to the larvae. Nurse bees also keep the brood cells clean and maintain the right temperature for the developing bees.

HOUSEKEEPERS: KEEPING THE HIVE TIDY

Worker bees also have the important job of keeping the hive clean and organized. They remove debris, dead bees, and other waste from the hive, ensuring a healthy environment for the colony. Housekeeping duties are usually performed by younger worker bees, who haven't yet started foraging.

BUILDERS AND REPAIRERS

Some worker bees are tasked with building and maintaining the honeycomb, the hive's essential structure made of beeswax. These bees produce wax from special glands in their abdomen, then shape the wax into hexagonal cells. The honeycomb is used to store honey, pollen, and brood, so keeping it in good condition is crucial for the colony's success.

GUARD BEES: PROTECTING THE HIVE

As worker bees get older, they may take on the role of guard bees. These brave ladies stand at the entrance of the hive, inspecting incoming bees to ensure they belong to the colony. Guard bees use their antennae to detect the unique pheromones of their hive-mates.

FORAGERS: COLLECTING FOOD FOR THE COLONY

The final and most well-known role of worker bees is foraging for food. Forager bees fly out in search of nectar, pollen, water, and propolis (a sticky plant resin). They use their incredible sense of smell and memory to locate flowers, and they communicate the location of food sources to their hive-mates using the waggle dance, as we learned in Chapter 7.

A WORKER BEE'S LIFE: A CYCLE OF HARD WORK

The life of a worker bee is a cycle of hard work and dedication to the colony. From nursing to foraging, these industrious ladies keep the hive running smoothly and ensure the survival of the colony. Their efforts are truly the backbone of the beehive.

Drones

Let's now focus on the often-overlooked members of the colony: the drones. These male bees may not be as busy as their female counterparts, but they play a crucial role in the survival of the species. So, let's get to know the drones and their unique purpose within the hive!

DRONE BASICS

Drones are the male bees in a colony, and they're larger and stockier than worker bees or the queen. They have large eyes that almost touch at the top of their head, which helps them with their primary duty - mating. Drones do not have a stinger, so they're unable to defend the hive or collect food.

A DRONE'S LIFE: LAID-BACK LIVING

The life of a drone is much more laid-back than that of a worker bee. Drones don't have many responsibilities within the hive, as they don't forage, build, or care for the brood. Instead, drones spend most of their time inside the hive, resting and waiting for their moment to shine.

Worker bees provide food for the drones, feeding them nectar and pollen. Drones also rely on the colony to keep them warm during cold weather, as they're unable to generate heat as efficiently as worker bees.

THE MATING FLIGHT: A DRONE'S MAIN MISSION

The primary purpose of a drone is to mate with a virgin queen bee, ensuring the continuation of the species. When a queen is ready to mate, she'll take a mating flight, attracting drones from nearby colonies. The drones will chase the queen, and the fastest and strongest drones will have the opportunity to mate with her in mid-air.

After mating, the drone's life comes to an end, as the process of mating is fatal for him.

THE END OF THE SEASON: A DRONE'S FAREWELL

As the cold weather approaches, the colony's resources become scarce. The worker bees, focused on the survival of the colony, will start to force the drones out of the hive, as they're no longer needed for mating and consume valuable resources. Sadly, the drones are unable to survive outside the hive without the support of the colony, and they will die.

Solitary bees

Unlike honeybees and bumblebees, solitary bees don't live in colonies. Instead, each female bee builds her own nest, lays her eggs, and gathers food for her offspring all by herself. Solitary bees don't produce honey or beeswax, but they are still important pollinators in their own right.

NESTING HABITS

Solitary bees have diverse nesting habits. Some species, like the mason bee, build nests in small holes or crevices, using mud, leaves, or other materials to create individual cells for their eggs. Others, like the leafcutter bee, cut small pieces of leaves to line their nests, which can be found in hollow plant stems or holes in wood.

CARING FOR THEIR YOUNG

Once a solitary bee has built her nest, she will lay an egg in each cell and provide a supply of pollen and nectar for her future offspring. After sealing the cell, she leaves the nest and will never see her babies hatch. The larvae will feed on the stored food, eventually transforming into adult bees and emerging from the nest to start the cycle all over again.

EFFICIENT POLLINATORS

While solitary bees might not create honey, they are still excellent pollinators. In fact, some solitary bees are even more efficient at pollination than honeybees! As they forage for nectar and pollen, they transfer pollen from one flower to another, helping plants to produce seeds and fruit.

Honey

In this chapter, we're going to explore the delicious and fascinating world of honey. From its production by hardworking bees to its many uses and benefits, honey truly is a remarkable substance. So, let's take a journey from flower to jar and learn all about this sweet treasure!

NECTAR TO HONEY: THE TRANSFORMATION

Honey starts its journey as nectar, a sweet liquid produced by flowers to attract pollinators like bees. Foraging worker bees visit flowers and use their long, tube-like tongues called **proboscises** to sip up the nectar. They store the nectar in a special part of their stomach called the **honey stomach**.

Back at the hive, the forager bee passes the nectar to a house bee through a process called **trophallaxis**. This involves transferring the nectar mouth-to-mouth, and it's during this exchange that enzymes in the bees' saliva begin to break down the nectar's complex sugars into simpler ones. This is the first step in transforming nectar into honey.

EVAPORATION STATION: THE HONEY-MAKING PROCESS

The house bee then deposits the partially-digested nectar into a honeycomb cell. To turn this nectar into honey, the bees need to reduce its water content. They do this by fanning their wings over the cells, creating airflow that evaporates the water and thickens the nectar.

Once the nectar has reached the right consistency, the bees cap the honey-filled cell with a layer of beeswax. This honey is now ready to be stored and used by the colony as a food source, especially during times when flowers are scarce.

HARVEST TIME: COLLECTING HONEY

Beekeepers harvest honey by carefully removing frames of honeycomb from the hive. They then uncap the cells by removing the thin layer of beeswax, allowing the honey to flow out. The frames are placed in a honey extractor, a machine that spins the frames, to extract the honey from the comb.

After extraction, the honey is usually filtered to remove any remaining beeswax particles or other debris. The honey is then ready to be bottled and enjoyed!

THE MANY USES OF HONEY

Honey isn't just a delicious natural sweetener; it's also packed with nutrients, antioxidants, and natural enzymes. On the right are just some of the many uses and benefits of honey.

Preservative
Honey's low water content and high sugar content make it a natural preservative, helping to stop the growth of bacteria and other microorganisms in foods like jams and fruit preserves.

Food and drink
Honey is a versatile ingredient in cooking and baking, adding natural sweetness and depth of flavor. It can also be used as a topping for toast, yogurt, or oatmeal, and as a sweetener in tea or other beverages.

Beauty treatments
Honey's moisturizing and antibacterial properties make it a popular ingredient in skincare products, like face masks, lotions, and lip balms.

Health remedy
Honey has been used for centuries to soothe sore throats and coughs. Its natural antimicrobial properties also make it useful for treating minor cuts and burns.

Pollination

You might already know that bees make delicious honey, but did you know they play an even more important role in our world? Bees are expert pollinators, helping plants to reproduce and grow the fruits and vegetables we love to eat. Let's explore the fascinating process of pollination and discover the amazing partnership between bees and plants.

WHAT IS POLLINATION?

Pollination is a crucial step in the reproduction process of flowering plants. It occurs when pollen, which contains the male reproductive cells, is transferred from the male part of the flower (the stamen) to the female part (the pistil) of the same or another flower. Once the pollen reaches the pistil, it fertilizes the ovules, eventually leading to the production of seeds and fruit.

THE BUZZ ABOUT BEES

Bees are nature's most efficient pollinators. When they visit flowers to collect nectar and pollen, they unintentionally transfer pollen from one flower to another. Their fuzzy bodies and the electrostatic charge they carry make it easy for pollen to stick to them.

As bees travel from flower to flower, some of the pollen rubs off onto the next flower they visit, completing the pollination process. Some plants even have special features, like bright colors and sweet scents, to attract bees and other pollinators.

WHY BEES MATTER

Bees play a vital role in pollinating the plants that make up a significant portion of our food supply. It's estimated that one-third of the food we eat relies on pollinators like bees. Without them, we would have fewer fruits, vegetables, nuts, and seeds, and the variety of foods available to us would decrease dramatically.

Remember, a healthy ecosystem relies on the teamwork of many different plants and animals. By learning about pollination and the vital partnership between bees and plants, we can better understand and appreciate the incredible connections that make our world so amazing. So next time you enjoy a delicious apple or a handful of almonds, take a moment to thank the bees for their hard work!

Threats to bees

AND HOW YOU CAN HELP

Our buzzing buddies are facing some tough challenges these days. From habitat loss to diseases and pesticides, bees are struggling to survive. But don't worry! There are things we can do to help protect these essential pollinators. Let's learn about the threats bees face and what we can do to make their lives a little easier.

HABITAT LOSS

As cities and towns grow, wild spaces where bees can find food and shelter are shrinking. With fewer flowers to forage and fewer places to nest, bee populations can decline. But there's good news! We can help by creating bee-friendly habitats in our gardens, parks, and neighborhoods.

CLIMATE CHANGE

Climate change affects bees, too! As temperatures rise and weather patterns shift, flowering plants may bloom at different times or not at all, leaving bees with less food. Droughts and floods can also destroy the plants bees rely on for nectar and pollen.

PESTICIDES AND OTHER DANGERS

Pesticides are chemicals used to control pests like insects, weeds, and fungi. Unfortunately, some of these chemicals can harm bees and other beneficial insects.

DISEASES AND PARASITES

Bees can fall victim to various diseases and parasites, like the Varroa mite, which can wipe out entire colonies. These tiny pests attach to bees and feed on their blood, weakening them and spreading deadly viruses.

What can <u>you</u> do to help?

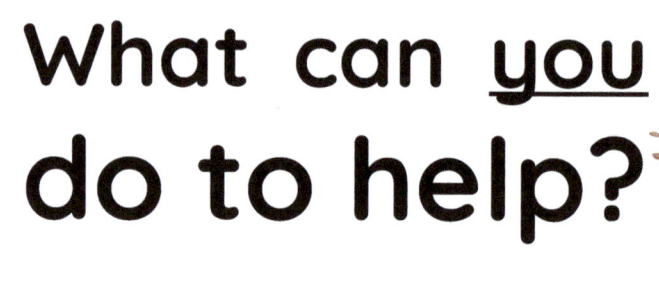

Everyone can play a role in ensuring a brighter future for bees.

Here are some ways you can contribute to their conservation and become a true Bee Hero!

PLANT A BEE-FRIENDLY YARD

Fill your garden with a variety of flowering plants that bloom throughout the year. This will provide a continuous source of food for bees.

Choose native plants, as they're best suited to support local bees.

SAY NO TO PESTICIDES

Avoid using harmful pesticides in your garden. If you need to control pests, opt for organic or bee-friendly alternatives.

CREATE A BEE HABITAT

Provide bees with nesting sites by leaving small piles of twigs, leaves, and brush in your garden. You can also install bee hotels or nesting boxes for solitary bees.

SUPPORT LOCAL BEEKEEPERS

Buy honey and other bee products from local beekeepers. This supports their efforts to maintain healthy bee populations and promotes sustainable beekeeping practices.

Bee Fun Facts

UN-BEE-LIEVABLE!

You've already learned so much about bees, but there's still more to discover! Prepare to dive into a treasure trove of even more fascinating and delightful fun facts about bees.

Afterwards, test yourself in the quiz!

Bees have five eyes: two large compound eyes and three smaller ocelli eyes.

• • •

Bees can see ultraviolet light, which helps them locate flowers and detect patterns that are invisible to humans.

• • •

The average bee can fly at speeds of up to 15 miles per hour (24 km/h).

• • •

Bees can fly in light rain, but heavy rain can make it difficult for them to maintain flight.

The foraging range of a bee is about 3 miles (5 km) from the hive, but they can travel up to 5 miles (8 km) if necessary.

• • •

A single bee colony can contain up to 60,000 bees at its peak.

• • •

Honeybees can recognize human faces.

• • •

Bees can count up to four.

• • •

Bees can learn and remember colors, shapes, and patterns, which helps them find food sources.

Bees can detect the Earth's magnetic field, which they use to navigate.

• • •

Bees can communicate with each other through vibrations.

• • •

Bees have been around for over 100 million years.

• • •

There are over 20,000 known species of bees worldwide.

• • •

Most bees are solitary, not living in colonies like honeybees and bumblebees.

THE ULTIMATE BEE BOOK

Some bees, like the mason bee, use mud to build their nests.

• • •

Honeybees are not native to the Americas; they were introduced by European settlers.

• • •

Bees are essential for pollinating about one-third of the world's food crops.

• • •

The honeybee is the official state insect of 17 U.S. states.

• • •

The smallest bee is the stingless bee, measuring only 2 millimeters in length.

The largest bee is the Wallace's giant bee, with a wingspan of up to 2.5 inches (6.3 cm).

• • •

Male bees in a colony are called drones, while female bees are called workers.

• • •

Bees don't sleep, but they do have periods of rest and inactivity.

• • •

A queen bee can lay up to 2,000 eggs per day.

• • •

Bees can get "drunk" from consuming fermented nectar.

Honeybees can be trained to detect explosives and diseases by recognizing specific scents.

• • •

The honeybee is the only insect that produces food eaten by humans.

• • •

Beeswax has been used for thousands of years for various purposes, including candle making and cosmetics.

• • •

Some bees, like the cuckoo bee, are "brood parasites," laying their eggs in the nests of other bee species.

Bees can recognize and remember the scent of their hive-mates.

• • •

Bees can fly as high as 13,000 feet (3,962 m) above sea level.

• • •

Bees can flap their wings up to 200 times per second.

• • •

Honey never spoils, and honey pots found in ancient tombs are still edible.

Worker bees can carry up to half their body weight in pollen or nectar.

· · ·

Bumblebees have hair on their eyes to help collect and sense pollen.

· · ·

Honeybees are responsible for pollinating around 80% of all fruit, vegetable, and seed crops in the U.S.

· · ·

Some flowers, like the snapdragon, have "landing strips" to guide bees toward their nectar.

· · ·

A foraging bee will visit between 50 and 100 flowers on a single trip.

Bees can sense a flower's temperature and prefer warmer flowers for nectar collection.

A honeybee's sense of smell is so precise that it can differentiate hundreds of different types of flowers.

Bees can get heatstroke, and some bees fan the hive to help cool it down.

Bees can adjust their body temperature by flexing their wing muscles, allowing them to fly in various weather conditions.

Bees have two stomachs: one for food and one specifically for storing nectar.

• • •

Bees have been known to chase away predators like bears, defending their hive even in the face of such formidable foes.

• • •

Some solitary bees, like the leafcutter bee, use pieces of leaves or flower petals to create their nests.

• • •

Beeswax from the hive has been used to create seals for important documents, like the 1215 Magna Carta.

Honeybees are used in a practice called **apitherapy**, where bee venom is used to treat conditions like arthritis and multiple sclerosis.

Some bees, like the Australian sugarbag bee, produce honey with unique flavors based on the plants they visit.

Honeybees have hair on their bodies to help collect pollen and keep them warm.

THE ULTIMATE BEE BOOK

The Bee Quiz

Were you paying attention?! Test your new bee knowledge!

1. What is the primary role of the queen bee in a colony?

2. Name the three types of bees found in a honeybee colony.

3. What is the main purpose of drones in a bee colony?

4   How many eyes does a bee have?

5   How do bees use their proboscis?

6   What is trophallaxis and why is it important in honey production?

7   How do bees turn nectar into honey?

8   What is the purpose of beeswax in a bee colony?

9   What is the main job of worker bees?

10   How do bees help in pollinating plants?

11   Bees can navigate using the Earth's magnetic field. True or false?

THE ULTIMATE BEE BOOK

12 How many known species of bees are there worldwide?

13 What are some uses and benefits of honey?

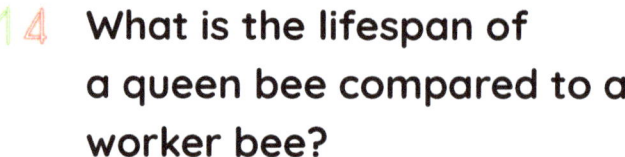

14 What is the lifespan of a queen bee compared to a worker bee?

15 What happens to drones at the end of the season?

16 How do bees adjust their body temperature for different weather conditions?

17 All drone bees are female. True or false?

18 Bees can detect different types of flowers through their sense of smell. True or false?

19 Name the smallest and largest known bee species.

20 What is the difference between solitary bees and social bees like honeybees?

21 How do beekeepers harvest honey from the hive?

THE ULTIMATE BEE BOOK

Answers

1. To lay eggs and produce offspring for the colony.
2. Queen, workers, and drones.
3. The main purpose of drones is to mate with a queen bee.
4. Five.
5. Bees use their proboscis to sip up nectar from flowers.
6. Trophallaxis is the process of transferring nectar mouth-to-mouth between bees.
7. Bees turn nectar into honey by adding enzymes to break down sugars and evaporating water to thicken the nectar.
8. Beeswax is used to build the honeycomb structure of the hive and cap honey-filled cells.
9. To forage for food, tend to the brood, build and maintain the hive, and defend the colony.
10. Bees transfer pollen from the male part of a flower to the female part, allowing fertilization and the growth of seeds or fruits.
11. True.
12. Over 20,000.

13. Food and drink, health, beauty treatments, and as a natural preservative.
14. A queen bee can live for several years, while a worker bee typically lives for just a few weeks.
15. Drones are expelled from the hive by worker bees.
16. They flex their wing muscles, generating heat or cooling themselves down as needed.
17. False.
18. True.
19. The smallest bee is the stingless bee, measuring only 2 millimeters in length, and the largest bee is the Wallace's giant bee, with a wingspan of up to 2.5 inches.
20. Solitary bees live and reproduce alone, while social bees like honeybees live in large colonies.
21. Beekeepers harvest honey by removing frames of honeycomb from the hive, uncapping the cells, and using a honey extractor to spin the frames and collect the honey.

Can you find all the words below in the word search puzzle on the right?

HONEY	SWARM	WORKER
POLLEN	NECTAR	MASON
BUMBLEBEE	QUEEN	POLLINATION

Bees Word Search

F	D	W	O	R	K	E	R	C	X	P	B
T	B	Q	Y	H	C	X	Z	H	N	O	N
R	F	U	V	C	O	Z	S	A	E	L	F
S	Q	D	M	B	G	N	K	D	C	L	D
Q	W	W	E	B	C	Q	E	N	T	I	S
S	K	A	G	F	L	U	S	Y	A	N	T
F	Q	D	R	C	B	E	R	S	R	A	E
H	W	Y	F	M	N	E	B	K	J	T	J
G	W	K	G	F	D	N	C	E	D	I	G
F	P	O	L	L	E	N	A	W	E	O	F
A	H	G	F	S	A	M	A	S	O	N	S
S	N	H	F	S	A	W	D	F	G	H	V

THE ULTIMATE BEE BOOK

Solution

		W	O	R	K	E	R		P
	B			H				N	O
		U			O			E	L
S		M			N			C	L
		W		B	Q	E		T	I
		A		L	U		Y	A	N
			R		E			R	A
			M		E	B			T
					N		E		I
		P	O	L	L	E	N		E	O
					M	A	S	O	N

Sources

Caron, D.M. & Connor, L.J. 2013. Honey Bee Biology and Beekeeping. Kalamazoo, MI: Wicwas Press.
Free, J.B. 1993. Insect Pollination of Crops. 2nd ed. London: Academic Press.

Grout, R.A. 1931. The Hive and the Honey Bee. Hamilton, IL: Dadant & Sons.

Hooper, T. 1997. Guide to Bees and Honey. 3rd ed. Wiltshire, UK: The Crowood Press.

Morse, R.A. & Hooper, T. 1985. The Illustrated Encyclopedia of Beekeeping. New York: E.P. Dutton.

Ransome, H. 2014. The Sacred Bee in Ancient Times and Folklore. Mineola, NY: Dover Publications.

Seeley, T.D. 2010. Honeybee Democracy. Princeton, NJ: Princeton University Press.

von Frisch, K. 1967. The Dance Language and Orientation of Bees. Cambridge, MA: Harvard University Press.

Wilson-Rich, N., Spivak, M., & Starks, P. 2014. Bee: A Natural History. Princeton, NJ: Princeton University Press.

Winston, M.L. 1987. The Biology of the Honey Bee. Cambridge, MA: Harvard University Press.

American Beekeeping Federation. 2023. [online] Available at: https://www.abfnet.org/ [Accessed 27 April 2023].

Bumblebee Conservation Trust. 2023. [online] Available at: https://www.bumblebeeconservation.org/ [Accessed 27 April 2023].

Honey Bee Health Coalition. 2023. [online] Available at: https://honeybeehealthcoalition.org/ [Accessed 27 April 2023].

Honeybee Centre. 2023. [online] Available at: https://www.honeybeecentre.com/ [Accessed 27 April 2023].
National Honey Board. 2023. [online] Available at: https://www.honey.com/ [Accessed 27 April 2023].

National Pollinator Garden Network. 2023. [online] Available at: https://www.pollinator.org/gardens [Accessed 27 April 2023].

Pollinator Partnership. 2023. [online] Available at: https://www.pollinator.org/ [Accessed 27 April 2023].
The Bee Cause Project. 2023. [online] Available at: https://www.beecause.org/ [Accessed 27 April 2023].

The Honeybee Conservancy. 2023. [online] Available at: https://thehoneybeeconservancy.org/ [Accessed 27 April 2023].

The Xerces Society. 2023. [online] Available at: https://xerces.org/ [Accessed 27 April 2023].

Dyer, A.G. & Chittka, L. 2004. 'Biological Significance of Distinguishing Between Similar Colors in Spectrally Variable Illumination: Bumblebees (Bombus terrestris) as a Case Study', Journal of Comparative Physiology A, 190(2), pp. 105-114.

Seeley, T.D. 2003. 'Consensus Building During Nest-site Selection in Honey Bee

You're Un-bee-lievable!

As our bee-utiful journey through the world of bees comes to an end, we hope you've enjoyed learning about these fascinating insects as much as we enjoyed sharing their story with you.

Your feedback means a lot to us, so we kindly ask you to **leave a review** on the platform where you purchased the book.

Your thoughts and experiences will help other readers discover the captivating world of bees and encourage us to continue creating engaging and educational content for all.

Thank you for your support!

ALSO BY JENNY KELLETT

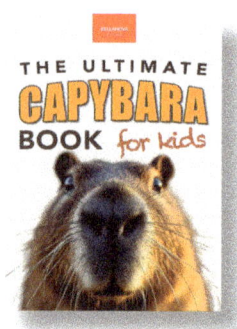

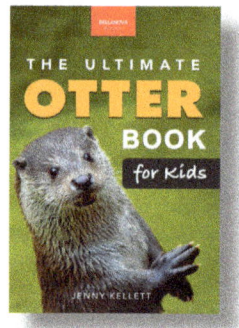

... and more!

Available at

www.bellanovabooks.com

and all major online bookstores.

www.ingramcontent.com/pod-product-compliance
Lightning Source LLC
LaVergne TN
LVHW050843080526
838202LV00009B/321